Orphic Wonder

KB Eliza

Copyright © 2024 by KB Eliza

www.kbelizawrites.com.au

Ponderings Publications Australia

PO Box 353, Leopold, Vic Australia 3224

No part of this book may be reproduced in any form or by any electronic or mechanical means, including information storage and retrieval systems, without written permission from the author or publisher.

HB ISBN: 978-0-6450309-8-3

PB ISBN: 978-0-6450309-7-6

PONDERINGS
PUBLISHING
AUSTRALIA

For Montanna
My life started with you my darling x

Contents

Introduction	xi
Reverie	1
Psalm for Self	3
Lullaby	4
Riot	7
Ballet of Slow Days	8
Very Very	10
The Story	11
Alignment	12
Education	13
Liberty	14
No Crumbs	15
Second Place	16
Good Girl	17
Thwart	19
The Atlas of You	20
Guest	21
Proof of Life	22
Benefactor	24
The Postman is a Stranger	25
True Journey	27
Double Choc Chip	28
Blue	30
Drop your shoulders	31
No Expectations	32
Star Scatter	33
What Lies Beneath	35
Stain	36
Prosper	37
Russian Doll	38
Impossible Things	40
On Hold	41

Love Makers	43
These Moments	44
Return to Sender	45
Stereo Hearts	46
Mindful	48
Borrower of Miracles	49
Oops	51
Failure to Launch	52
You Are	54
Rejection	55
Forever	57
Crumble	58
Admission	60
Liar	61
Stages	63
Tonic	64
Cloak	65
Pirate	66
Gravitate	67
Crucible	68
Depth Call	69
Transcend	70
Kiss and Whispers	71
What Do You See?	72
Time Jumper	74
Little Stranger	75
No	77
Trauma Echo	78
Photon	80
The Pauper called Ego	81
FOMO	83
Little One	84
Cave	85
Word War	86
Reach	87
The Party is Over	88
Courage	89
Visitor	90

Word Trade	91
Binary	92
Boundless	93
Phoenix in Hiding	94
Breath	95
Faith	96
Holdings	98
Edify	99
Dogma	100
Wild Love	101
Axiom	103
Feast	104
Elixir	105
Farewell for Now, with Love	106
Lemon Juice	107
Verbosity	108
Converge	109
Hide and Seek	110
Stars Collide	111
Due North	112
Boundless	113
Wherefore Art Thou?	114
Matrix	115
Potent	116
Gold Crush	117
Sleepwalking	118
Toxic Shedding	120
The Architect	121
Sticky Fingers	123
Limerence	124
Damage	125
Old Foe	126
Witnesses	128
Platform 22	129
Loops	130
Day of Frogs	131
Neenish Tarts	133
Teenage Love	134

Blue Freckles	135
Last Words	137
Telephone	138
Ignition	139
Dilute	140
Burn Away	141
Guideposts	142
My Corinthian	143
Seriously	144
Tug of War	145
Storm	146
Longwinded	147
Keep Your Hands to Yourself	148
SShhhh	150
Haunted House	151
Treehouse	153
Ambrosia	154
Romance of Words	155
Peanut Butter and Honey	156
Comedian	158
The Land of Grandmother	159
Toe the Line	161
Secret place	162
Dreaming	163
Midnight Feast	164
No Roses Today	165
Alphabet Soup	167
Truth Shaker	168
Upside Down	170
Contortionist	171
Count	172
Child of Mine	173
Notes	174
The Roar	175
Bin Day	177
Burleigh Heads	178
Visitor	180
Salt and Honey	181

Flattery	183
Absurdity	184
Ribbons	185
Grip	186
Inquisitive	187
Rose Coloured Glasses	188
Incite	190
Seasons	191
Virus	192
Fishing	193
Passports Please	194
Checklist	195
Control Panel	196
All Silk and Whispers	197
Margins	199
Doorways	200
Vase	202
Ride of Your Life	203
Too Late	205
The Velocity of I AM	206
Ashes to Ashes	208
About the Author	209

Introduction

Dear Reader,

This book of poetry is presented in a different format from many others. The lack structured sections is intentional. You can open it at any page and find a message that resonates with you.

The poems are a mixed bag, from the nostalgia of childhood to the experience of facing the many messy, painful and joyful moments in life. Living a life of metaphysical enquiry punctuated by the curious debacle of mortality looming and neurodiversity -means my life is never boring.

As I chose each one, I noticed a theme of the feminine and faith underpinning many of them. May you find one, sit with it and feel it deep in your bones.

As Maya Angelou said, 'We are more alike, my friends, than we are unalike.'

Introduction

Blessings, KB Eliza

Reverie

Orphic wonder,
Who tends to your wounds?
Your bandaged intent?
The pus seeps out
The stench of poor choices
A choir of social voices
Screech and break glass
Shards stick into the thickness
Of your thighs
Cutting hanging breasts
Stretched belly
Scarred.
You are a story
One to be told over eons
Scars, the fruits of battle
Your legs,
Strong.
Your chest,
Mighty,
Ancient.

KB Eliza

Your choices;
Chapters
In a universe designed
For adventures
Wars fought, earned and won.
Bury your dead.
Clean your wounds,
Sing your reverie.

Psalm for Self

Do unto me as I would do unto others.

Lullaby

Take your dishy darlings
Throw them to the depths
Collect your fetching falsities
Crush them into crumbs
Don't fight the slumber, baby
The time for affliction is done.

Does my truth bring an ache?
Make you toss and turn?
Does my lullaby provoke?
Make your vexed lip curl?

Retch those puckered words,
Your squeamish symphony
Cut the barbed wire wit
Hold that hauteur down
Close your covert eyes
Purge the tarnished gown

Does my love burn your skin?

Orphic Wonder

Make you shiver and shake?
Does my kindness insult?
Make your gusto break?

I'll mystify your stout logic,
Your fury will unfurl
Tranquillise that torment
Turn your poison into wine
Relax your life, beloved
Everything is going to be fine.

Riot

Riot and revelation can ensue when two worlds collide and meld into one. Or, they may remain shattered, ensnared and a mystery. The choice is yours.

Ballet of Slow Days

Villainous time is ticking,
stern limitation.
I walk a lunar lullaby
on cold grass, tickling
my warm living toes.

Under the mighty gaze
of one who holds all answers,
yet my soul is no marionette,
no strings pull at my freedom.

Time, in her unflinching deceit,
leads me to a dark forest of two paths,
seven days to live or die,
three months to say Goodbye,
a numeral noose of numbers.

A handful of days
to distil a bottle of memories,
labelled LIFE,

Orphic Wonder

a mead that tastes now like privilege.

Surgery, steely sterility,
saws, plates, screws, metallic
blading through the essence of my being,
delicate machetes, intricate and powerful,
gambling with the highest stakes.

A cluster of ticking moments
to gather my loves.
The ballet of slow days,
languid hours
drowning slowly with the rising tide
of crumbling fate.

Earnest prayers from my soul,
a request to murder fear,
liquid whispers fall down my face,
faith bubbles and bursts.

The enigma of surrender,
a vine, twirling helix, green embrace,
Flourishing self; you are felt.

Hope corrupts the darkness,
I hold her high, a lantern bright,
to guide me to bed,
held in hands divine, unseen and unheard.

Very Very

I thought you were the moon, so far away and so bright. Slipping in and out of view. But I didn't have a telescope, and I'm no astrologer. When you were full I could see your face, a slight turn and I swear I saw your smile. Was is a trick of the light? What I would give for us to eclipse at a time that meets our schedules. We don't want to put the world in darkness, or blind them with our very very, shiny love. We truly are cosmic aren't we?

The Story

We can go the road alone.
But when we do not comprehend
we are here for a time to learn,
to feel and create,
to experience;
we will exercise falsities with good intentions.
When we hold the teacher close,
simplicity and joy join the adventure,
and fear is replaced with faith.
The world becomes a momentary adventure
in the story of eternity.

Alignment

We can love those not in alignment from a distance, but the soul journey with those who rise to the light will help us on our way.

Education

This person may not have learned
the lesson yet,
Perhaps they are not fully awake.
They may have left with their education,
one remains, circling the classroom.
Thank you for releasing this soul
to follow their path.
Love consistently from a distance,
and understand;
one day, they will see you,
know you.
You will both smile.
The student and teacher are in session.

Liberty

Liberty rises when the toxicity of others is shed, and only love remains.

No Crumbs

A cookie for breakfast.
laughing until I ache,
- dancing to loud music.

Bare feet stomping
- am I singing?
at the top of my lungs
not hitting a single note.

Drinking from the best crystal,
adorned in flowing skirts
- and bangles

Watching the sun rise,
an intoxicating kiss
- I am Alive.

Second Place

Ego takes second place to divine will.

Good Girl

Good girl, good girl,
where are you now?
Now that you've lost your manners,
your pleasing was for others,
your thank you's weren't returned.

Good girl, good girl,
why don't you brush your hair?
It's so frizzy and unkempt,
why don't you put some makeup on?
Those eyes need to be bigger.

Good girl, good girl,
why don't you have a career?
Why don't you start a family?
You'll feel better when you're skinny.

Good girl, good girl,
don't tell them what you think.

KB Eliza

Don't raise your voice or get angry—
That's not what good girls do.

Thwart

Vulnerability is the antithesis of thwarted independence.

The Atlas of You

Draw your map of consciousness,
your awakening journey.
You are animated stardust;
you are quantum and momentum.
There is a vast land to discover,
the Atlas of you awaits.
So chart your course,
make adjustments,
and smile; you are emerging.

Guest

People arrive if you invite the idea of them in.

Proof of Life

Rails gripped, white knuckled,
- one more step,
just one movement.
What was simple, now an unruly vagrant matrix.

Automated miracles bestowed long ago,
now meandering
- sinew,
Flying like leaves in a tempest.

Sweat, slippery and telling,
- trickles down my spine.
Sweet relief explodes into my smile.

Steady cadence of perspiration,
concentration
- proof of life.
My foot moves, I have tamed the wild.
Victorious motion

Orphic Wonder

- you are a dream weaver

There will be dancing again.

Benefactor

Your broken parts are the benefactors of wisdom.

The Postman is a Stranger

A musical knock at the door,
familiar and known.
I'm here to deliver a parcel,
is she home?
I am her; you know me.

Revulsion scatters across his face,
like freckles.
What happened? You were so pretty.

                    Brain surgery.

Pity floats through the screen,
like dour tobacco smoke.
Awkward silence,
too much pause.

                We are strangers now, unwoke.

KB Eliza

Parcels once handed over
with a smile,
are left at the door,
no enthused encore.

                The music is gone.

True Journey

Travelling far beyond the capacity of feet is the true journey my friend.

Double Choc Chip

Ice-cream melted
down his arm
as he choked back tears of deep sadness.
The grief hit him in the middle
of a vanilla double choc dip,
the hardened chocolate now a brown rivulet,
sticking to the hairs on his arms.
What would become of them?
Who would tend to the herbs, picked
and steeped
for tea in China cups painted with peonies?
Who would he be without her
laugh and soft snores?
His secret teller,
future maker,
holder of crazy dreams.
His?
- not his.
She was fate's now,
and was he hers?

Orphic Wonder

The world felt flat
and vast
like a slow-moving dance
in mud,
- a bad dream.
Before the void
could swallow him,
he wiped the sticky sadness
with his sleeve
and remembered
- to ring the plumber.

Blue

I remember seeing you across the room and wondering what it was exactly that drew me to you. I do remember your eyes, you looked friendly and warm and people were laughing at what you were saying.

Drop your shoulders

Is your shoulder soft and golden?
Or is it a hard sharp edge?
Do you open your curiosity,
or close it, like a book you've already read?

Too hard to read, once open,
back turned, with tired eyes,
you stretch your pointed finger,
With a heart truly *weaponised*.

Shaking hands, once steady,
meanings you want to forget,
stumbling steps, once agile,
broken ankles carrying regret.

Loosen your love a little,
let it out, it needs to breathe.
Those shoulders need to drop,
- it's time for you to receive.

No Expectations

Why seek a resolution with an expectation that has no form?

Star Scatter

Stars scattered like seconds,
a multitude of opportunity,
sparkling in our eyes edge,
dazzling us with inspiring awe,

Waiting to be grasped,
Wanting to be captured,
elusive fireflies fleeting,
possibility dangled by that
Old Master Time
- the watchful keeper.

Our thoughts cannot steal us,
away from this magnificent night,
from the majesty of moments
- in the polarising sky of now

As we orbit around our days,
what might our lives sparkle?

KB Eliza

Telescopic hearts, bringing us closer
to the universe
- holding the ones we love.

What Lies Beneath

The flow and ebb of energy can be elusive and hard to understand. But this is part of what lies beneath the ordinary.

Stain

The grimy stain of truth
The grimy stain of truth
- upon the skirts of a lie,
I rub and twist, rub and twist,
- under water without magic.

None will take the horror,
none will shift the ruin.
Bare legs, scratched and naked,
under the curious gaze of others,
- haunted.

Scissors sharpened by secrets,
cut away the tainted blot.
A needle threaded with new.
I weave and pull, pull and weave.
Stitching a cloak of luster,
with twill of pearl and gold,
- the colour of my heart.

Prosper

You will know prosperity in spirit when your thoughts are tending to your heart.

Russian Doll

Maiden, sweet maiden,
I cannot be you.
You were once the sweet part of me,
tender, fresh, and new.
Where your smooth skin sits,
my wisdom now adorns.
My freedom is liberation,
like new shoes not yet worn.

These wrinkles are the markings of a warrior,

have you not seen one before?

Let us sit by the scented fire,
I will show you how your bow needs string.
I will teach you the notes for music you will make,

the world waits for you to sing.

Orphic Wonder

We will tap our feet as they merge,
you can make me smile with your dream making,
perhaps I may season them with tales,

       under the stars of our awakening.

Impossible Things

When you love with all your heart and ask for nothing in return it is a beautiful impossible thing.

On Hold

On messages, we roll
Around in circles,
Dancing to music
We didn't create.

Crashing in waves,
Goodbye to the storm, I scream.
Goodbye to the chaos.

Pierce me with your point,
Or make one, either way,
I am tired
Of hidden messages in your voice.

To my ears the gesture rings
A bell too sweet to repeat
Sacrificial sentiment, too heavy
To carry for the likes of you.

From off the floor, I step

KB Eliza

Into a dawn of my own
Making.

These new moves,
Away from the tangled mess
We made,
into new Music,
Made sweeter with faith
I trust
My decisions, actions,
From intuitive reason
I drink.

Love Makers

You cannot sit alone with your scrapes and broken bones, in a dark room petrified by fear. You were made for connection.

These Moments

These moments, these stories, these memories—
the sound of our life flicking over
like pages
being read too fast.
I don't want to skim the details;
I want the hook,
I want the red herring,
and damn it, I want my happy ending.
they say you can't take it with you,
but I will take each one and stitch them
into my skin—
These moments, these stories, these memories.

Return to Sender

For love not returned is not love not truly received.

Stereo Hearts

Our souls whisper
Quietly, tiptoeing
Through the bracken
Sharpened by life's devices
Unplugged from our source
Of self, of destiny or fate

Each one a mystery
To be solved or ignored
By our inquisitive nature
Seeking rain in drought
Dirt dusted and cracked
Scripts, cryptic and ancient

Crafted stories in books
Brush against our spines
Tingling, shivering
In the cold night of thoughts
Ruminating, repeating
Lines over and over

Orphic Wonder

Begging discharge
Lightning and liberation
From mute to stereo
Stomping of one lost
Now found in the truth
Of our noisy hearts.

Mindful

When someone is stuck in irrational thought, don't question their reality. Listen and observe with compassion.

Borrower of Miracles

Above the white noise,
Do you feel my voice?
Can you sense my faith?
The essence of my choice?

Decisions, decisions,
Which is the stronger my love?
Or are you frozen by fear-
-compounded by the loudness of others?

My smile is so familiar,
Yet my sweet hair gone,
Scars now slash my sunken skull
Who is this monster- imposter?

I am not missing,
I have not vanished,
Let your panic be swallowed by awe
For you are witnessing, my child,
What it means to be restored.

KB Eliza

Feel the love I have for you,
Let it drown out the rumble of horror,
It is me little one,
I am the borrower of miracles
And memories are ours to be made.

Oops

What happens when that which you crave; becomes an act of self-betrayal?

Failure to Launch

Fear fails to feel,
falling from your favour,
landing on my feet.
Too tired to climb again,
blistered, bulging, bruised,
stalls and floats,
scorching a hole
in my trust in us both,
burning the hurt to cinders.
I may warm my hands to
the flames I light my torch with insight,
finding my way.

I am raised into life.

Paint your timber, polish your crystal ball,
while I trek an adventure,
watching a new dawn
in promised places.
For life is filled with tasks,

Orphic Wonder

but nothing does it quite like love.

Memories for one aren't as strong,
punctuated with another's laugh and shared meaning,
is what makes new memories a gift
to treasure and hold close.

'Remember when' doesn't exist in a room for one -
it's an echo in an empty room.
Loneliness is a terrible place,
a space of gaps and echoes.
The warmth of another heart close to yours
is different from loving solitude for you, you enjoy.
I saved a place for you,
I waited so very long.
Do these love letters have invisible ink?
These blank pages on my desk.
An unpredictable and dark, charming mind,
disputing the dark inner argument,
lighting a fiery fuse.
Tame the blame.
Hollow voice,
broken, I have woken.
Silence is violent.

You Are

You hurt, and you have felt love, you have felt fear, you have felt care, you have felt joy. You are a Life.

Rejection

Do you need to remind me of who I am
with fancy clothes and the respectful nod
from others?
The doer of good deeds and friendly words,
well placed in the crowded room
of influence?

Do I really believe your whining voice,
begging me for food, so hungry?
'Don't discard me,' you plead.
'No one will know our value,
we will be discarded, abandoned.'

Do not drop that smile,
don't you dare complain!
Your needs are demands, and shame on you.
Be of service, be for others, be, be, be.

Wear your martyr like a filigree brooch
so everyone knows who we are;

KB Eliza

a good soul, a loving person always there,
never asking or expecting.

No.
You are a part of me, old friend,
but I no longer drink tea at this table.
In this land of labels,
I will not be catalogued or kept in check.
That harping harness pulling me this way
and that.

Farewell, dear Ego, today I tip my hat.
Adieu, for now.
I am leaving you at the door,
the invite was for one.

Forever

Hold on because the hurt won't last. Forever does not exist here.

Crumble

Leaves fall, without despair, to an earth that holds them
Is this the choice I must make?
Fierce fight for control?
If the soul only knows to fight to survive
Letting go feels like drowning,
An inconceivable transaction for a promise of peace
From an unseen hand.

The veil is lifted, and I am spellbound
Captured voluntarily
Such is my surrender in this solitude,
Divinely spun dance of circumstance,

Doubt crumbles and I drop from the hard
Platform of fear to
Grass, soft and comforting, holding me
Mossy wisdom's embrace

Majestic mystical movement

Orphic Wonder

Stirs and swells in my soul
Bewildering familiarity blinding
My downcast sorrow; a deluge
Now held tight in mighty refuge.

Admission

No person can pass this gate of protection without the admission price; truth.

Liar

Strife pulled the knife.
It wasn't me, I promise,
But I hid it just the same.
Is the concealment worth it?
A comet threatens our still night.
To protect you now,
I adore your calm,
Filling our days like a tonic.
Do I trust you?
With my life, yes!
I have not told all that consumes,
For fear it will consume you too.
This secret is my armour
Around us, what we were,
What we might become.
What would we be,
Allowed to be friends,
To know each other still?
My love is stronger

KB Eliza

Then the truth you do not know.
My omission is not wrong or right,
It is my burden to carry,
The weight a small pierce to keep
Our love alive.

Stages

Transcend the past; it only exists in the depths of your memory seeking a new stage to play out the unhealed.

Tonic

I am not a broken jug
Or the 'such a shame' cliche
I am a story in motion
Where trauma and victory collide
The hand of God has touched me
Can you see it materialise?
My skin radiates with promise
It shines with unfiltered hope,
For there cannot be a harvest of light
Without the crippling tonic of growth.

Cloak

Control is a cloak of self-deception.

Pirate

Concealing my meaning
striving to divide,
poking around my words,
picking out pieces of sky.

But it's an ocean in motion,
crashing against the shore,
gifting shells of vulnerability
- curiously seeking more.

I'm not your puzzle piece,
your felted worn bookmark,
a sentence to be sliced
- The antagonist in your lark.

Close your mouth, shut your lies.
Pause your process, open your mind.
Stories are treasures, so take caution
before your ink has dried.

Gravitate

When we emit our highest frequency of love, those around us will gravitate toward this or be repelled.

Crucible

Discarded to be discovered,
Abused to aligned,
Halted to protected,
Injury to ingenuity
Grief to gratitude
Rejection to opportunity,
Misunderstood to manifested
Clouded into clarity
The blueprint is nimble,
You are an alchemist,
Gather your tools,
Uncover faith,
It's time to distil your destiny.

Depth Call

If you look into darkness too long, it sings to you. Calling you into its depths. Pain seeking consciousness. It does not want you; it needs you to feed from. What is the lesson?

Transcend

Once, I knew every curve
Now, I don't know your shape
The hold is so tight
Now you fight
Is my love a cage to escape?
I run away to places
On empty promises, I glide
Your bite stings like a swarm
Touch now cold, warmth is gone
What place is safe to hide?
What name shall I call now?
I drop to the sand
Without hope, without demand
Who shall I say you are?
It doesn't feel like *friend*.
As the word falls to my heart, I smile,
I shall call you; **Transcend**.

Kiss and Whispers

Wounds can be closed and filled with the golden tonic of self-love. So, pat your skin, kiss your wrist and whisper every word you ever wanted to hear. Your core will believe you, and your soul will be thankful.

What Do You See?

Do I reek of middle-aged privilege?
Do you like my shiny boots?
These boots must be designer,
Designed for these feet—
These feet that learned to walk again
From the wrong side of the tracks.
What do YOU see?

These boots come off at the door
Of my five-bedroom home.
My house, sweet house, I love,
Because this house is not a caravan
Where no one knows our names,
Hidden away from the tyranny
Of fists and fear.
What do YOU see?

Do you like my hair? My long red locks,
Curled to perfection.
My hair grew unruly, it seems,

Orphic Wonder

From the bald tufts imposed
By chemical warfare to save my life,
When these feet could not move,
When these eyes could not see.
Tell me, friend, what do you REALLY see?

Time Jumper

Do you ever feel like you could poke a hole in the air with your finger and peek into your other lives?

Little Stranger

Little stranger, I have known forever,
each little finger holds mine.
New eyes, so wise,
shine back at me.
Familiar, fragile, divine.
A blank slate with hidden codes,
the overwhelm and fear
enveloped in a love.

Relying on me for survival,
to be the teacher on
how to live, love, and be free.
To know what it is to be
and feel beautiful in a world
that makes it impossible.

I cannot break you with projections
and protections.
I cannot let you win everything,
entitled, jilted, stilted.

KB Eliza

When I want to give you the world,
wrapped in a bow.

Be tough, be brave, be vulnerable.
Close the door,
open up wide.
Here comes the food;
ten years later, it will be toxic
when you remind me of the mistakes.

We learn together, as I have never
been a teacher, but I will always be
Mother.

No

I should have said no to you, but I was scared it would disconnect us.

Trauma Echo

Lurid injury, stinging my lips
Purple, blue shadows
Reign down hues of hate
Flashing eyes
Wide, surprised.

Your melodrama darkness
Slipping around my throat
Take leave,
Novel enemy of the past.

I'll blow you away like smoke
Rings float from lips, now full
Of promise.
I'll show you **mine**.

Show me your **sorry**,
I'll show you my heart that
Flaps in the wind
Like a torn tent door

of crimson agony.

Show me your **good time**,
I'll show you the scars
On my soul
Where the scab won't heal
And the slice thickens.

Show me your **horror**
And I will show you what grace
Really looks like:
Divine and mighty
-Born again

I take the gaping canvas scraps
And stitch them into a coat
I will mould the blemish you left
Into a brand,
It will say **Forgiveness**.

Photon

Infinity, quark, photon, atom, laughter and patterns. Mysterious? Yes. Unfathomable? Often. Are we in co-creation with God? This is a question worthy of asking. We might get an answer.

The Pauper called Ego

Stroke me, hold me
Don't be mad
Show me your love,
Mercy.
My arms enfold you as I swallow
My rage, my pride
I suffocate you and draw a map.
I call in healers, and you
Gobble them up like a starving orphan
You are full now
You are plump
Drained of my life force
I ask if you might share some
- Just a morsel.
You cry; how can you want what's mine?
You look to the heavens; how can she be
so greedy?
I need to stay fed.
I crawl to the water's edge

KB Eliza

Unbelieving, in denial
God lifts my chin as I lick at the mud,
And says you shall starve no more.

FOMO

Will you miss out because they want more?

Little One

Little one left alone
Now standing in grown-up clothes
Stamping feet
Hot tears and *Go away*!
Plastered on every wall
Little one left alone
We are not there any more
You are big, and the danger is over
You are fresh and new
You belong.

Cave

Illusions hold us in a cave; we can find a way out.

Word War

Can't go back
Can't go forward
Can't stand still
Can't cry out
Can't say No
Can't say Me
Can't ask Why
Only in the land of demand.
Other territories await you,
Ones with promises sweet
Wings grow where words once sat
The love grows where hurt once festered
Here there are no T's
There are no apostrophes
Here, now, yes.

Reach

Yesterday and tomorrow could squeeze us between reaching hands that cannot touch. Such is the timing between misperceptions and clarity...

The Party is Over

Blow out the candle
Switch off the lights
Turn the music off
Agape has flown away
The clanging bells were too loud
Ice melted
Water soured over hours
Bloodshot eyes and memories
Too much
The diamond became a rock
Too heavy to carry
We shall sleep now
Tomorrow, we start anew
With quiet, calm
Gentle movements,
Without the crowd and cheer
Agape might return
Timid but yearning
Sweeter to the touch.

Courage

True courage is in surrender.

Visitor

He visits in a dream
Pulls me into his heart
Tells me the future is bright
Promises me the hurt is old
Every cell in my body
Lighting up, filling
No more empty spaces
No more shadows in halls
I wake up
I remain in his hold
The dream plunged into reality
Or reality into night
I am awakened either way.

Word Trade

Trade the words inflamed, beaten, and swollen for the beautiful beast of acceptance, joy and humour.

Binary

Why do you use words
to capture an identity
In a bottle made of lead?
He, She, Them, They
Want to belong
Want to be seen
But a flame with no name
is extinguished
You, with your words
bound in rules
Of what is, what isn't
What if this is an invitation?
Not to calamity but to stretch above?
Evolving into *'I see you'*
Evolution isn't easy, baby
Take a breath
Get curious
Be Kind.

Boundless

Love separate from want is boundless; there is no lack of supply.

Phoenix in Hiding

Smashed my heart
Tore it apart
With bared unintentional teeth
Weaponry built behind a fortress
Where weak mouths are taped shut
God knocks at the door as you ignore
Plunged
Into darkness
You are crumpled
You are humbled
You surrender
You take bandages and hold the shame close
Like a candle
Warming caliginous corners
It doesn't want to be seen
But the candle turns to wildfire
Clearing the path
For permission to live
Without the burden of regret or a hung head.

Breath

Do you remember when we laughed so hard we couldn't breathe? Breath is overrated.

Faith

Evaluating character takes time.
It's okay to protect yourself.
All earthly things will fail us,
for there will be days when
events unfold beyond comprehension,
when pain feels unbearable.

In these moments,
our understanding of **God**,
of who **He** is,
and how deeply **She** loves us,
becomes our rest.
We place our weary heads upon **Them**.

How do we live it out?
We simply start.
We live our belief
each time we choose to trust Home,
instead of trying to control, or avoid.
Despite our fears,

when we use our spiritual gifts
to impact others, or not,
our soul grows.

A lifelong pursuit
of closeness to God.
I don't know how this will turn out,
but I trust You.

For we live by faith,
not by sight.
By grace,
we have been saved,
not from ourselves,
not from good deeds.

It is a blessing from God,
not by works,
so no one can boast.
For a present not earned,
is no longer a gift,
but a reward.

Holdings

The wonder you find in others is a mirror shining back the elements you hold inside.

Edify

The cardinal anguish of the feminine
Screams across the waves
Weeping at the stolen light
Grieving the stolen masculine
Praying for it to return
Rise up, rise up

Feminine arise
Take your place
Feel the crescendo
There is no grace like it
It is time to shine your violet light
Smashing the lies to oblivion

Fierce warriors with gentle hearts will
Pierce the misguided shame
It has no place in the light
Balance; you are loved, you are wanted.

Dogma

Dogma and the stumbling malevolence of ego tend to lean towards chaos under the banner of deliverance.

Wild Love

You called me; I am scared.
Fearful of leaving solid ground.
Courage is needed—a lion's roar.

You wait for me,
promising hope
and a love to fill the vacuum left
in my scarred heart.

No human can do this.
You listen, not judge.
You know my essence.
You see under the trauma and call
to my primal ferocity,
borne from my mother and hers and that long line
of suffering,
teeming with sacrifice,
with love, dreams, and expression.

KB Eliza

Claim your nakedness and scream over the rage
of a lost voice.
Your time has come,
wild love.

Axiom

Mindset or madness, axiom or paradox?

Feast

Will we eat the feast prepared
Or will we sit beneath the table,
Begging for a taste?
Parched, poisoned, pierced
Licking gravy from plates
Of guests with golden watches
When no one is watching
There is no manna here.
No mortal can fill the void, and starvation
Divinity, numinous and never-ending
A constant stream of love
Separate from energy,
Once you taste its juicy fruits,
You will yearn again.

Elixir

Find the elixir in jars of like-minded folk in a world that prickles our skin with goosebumps.

Farewell for Now, with Love

When the words don't match the eyes
When promises disappear
When understanding is absent
And in its place lies expectation,
Wish them well with honour
They are finding their way -away from you
It's all going to be okay.

Lemon Juice

Reliance is a word that springs a leak in our ego. Helpless is a word that sits on the tongue like lemon juice.

Verbosity

Grow, stretch, love, be.
Weep, mourn, shout, run
Dance, sing, smile, laugh
Break, mend, born, transform
The humanity you were made for.

Converge

When we lower our energy to make ourselves and others feel at ease, we no longer converge into the synchronistic masterpiece that is our life. Belonging is necessary, but make sure you belong where you can shine at the highest frequency possible.

Hide and Seek

Peppered fractals are the clues
I leave for you in your scattered discontent.
Starlight to cosmos, skin cell to fingerprint
A weft in the quantum fabric
Let the treasure hunt begin.

Stars Collide

Perhaps we are the ancestors of stars colliding, an explosion vast and wonderful.

Due North

Elusive ocean of origin
Depths haunting us so!
We must sail from fragility
Tie up the boats and row!

We traced the path of the stars
They bellowed, 'Due North!'
Savage usurper evading us
Grab the science; set forth!

Raise the masts of identity
Our narrative is leaking
Hide the maps and golden plans
Confinement of proof is creaking!

To the depths, we sink aghast,
Alas no decoding of this creation
What is that? A rescuer!
Why, it's the swell of illumination.

Boundless

Archaic beliefs are the masters we must outsmart to unmask the potential of a boundless future.

Wherefore Art Thou?

Peace, Peace?
Where is this mischievous trickster,
eluding my grasp?
Ephemeral, vixen,
objectified.

First comes the alchemy,
then she will arrive unannounced, fleeting,
a welcome visitor.
Sit in her presence, enjoy her.
She may stay forever,
but she will never wear out her welcome.

Matrix

When we ignore our path and follow another's patterns in life, we enable them to make the same mistakes twice. We may believe we support; we might call it love. We might call it compassion. But herein lies the problem. We break our essence when we follow another's matrix. We betray ourselves unintentionally.

Potent

The flesh needs and longing begins.
The tension flexes between,
Potent, calm and grounded,
surrender and trust,
No longer an infant in recoil,
But a force of service
that seeks to lift the world up
and closer to home.

Gold Crush

The energy you externalise is precious. Refrain from diluting it or reducing and wasting your energy. Your life force is a precious soul commodity; trading it for ego and vanity is crushing gold and sweeping it away like dust. You are formidable; you are.

Sleepwalking

She believes she is nothing while they sleep
They believe they are everything
She discovers that she is a queen
They are all jesters walking in kings' clothes,
Tattered.
The only way forward is redemption,
She does not offer punishment
She produces a key to unlock the shackles
So, eyes may be opened,
Minds made pure and life made free
But instead, they make a fire from the small
twigs of her heart.
Redemption? They scoff.
Naught can be made with such folly,
We must warm our hands; we enslaved
money-makers,
They cry when their fingers are scorched,
The money is gone,
Remorse, remorse! They cry.

Orphic Wonder

Too late, the sleepwalkers awaken.
There is no turning back,
She smiles knowingly
Their healing starts now.

Toxic Shedding

Liberty rises when the toxicity of others is shed, and only love remains.

The Architect

I'm stuck.
I am stuck.
Bile rises up.
Heart races.

Turning, turning.
Stop, please stop.
Please, someone, stop this flow of blood from my heart.
The dam has broken, sliding into the mud,
drowning out reason.
Please, no more.

Thoughts of others invade,
I, like a secret voyeur,
watch that which only seeks to hurt me.
Why does my riven imagination drift?
A ragged wretch in need of saving.
I bend my knee, and with my plea, I am spent.

The Architect sits beside me,

KB Eliza

an unseen hand, an unseen hold.
'Are you finished yet, child?
Have you worn yourself out?
Who imposes this suffering?
Do you believe I would ever want this for you?'

'You call my name and believe me to be a puppeteer of cruelty?
Why would you ask to be saved by a master?
Only a slave to the world can think these thoughts.'
The Architect reminds me of the creation of love.

'Take gentle breaths, and let me cut the ties
that bite into your skin and soul.
You are saved.
You are living.
You do not need to succumb to a world that seeks to capture you.
I don't condemn you. I free you.
You are my beloved.'

Sticky Fingers

Our projections are held fast by the sticky fingers of history. Institutions and perceptions should not rob us of a curiosity that may yet offer an adventure. We hold in our hands an invitation to surpass the mundane and experience the profound.

Limerence

Hope set in motion makes my being
thrum to the music not yet discovered.
Its melody feels like a whisper
through the trees from a party
in a faraway place.

I want to join in and dance
beneath the night sky.
I must wait my turn
while preparations are made.

This limerence life can offer,
after destruction,
is intoxicating.
I take a seat and wait patiently,
enjoying the gentle pulse.

Damage

Unconditional love is the separation of expectation, need and energy. When we love unconditionally, the unsigned contracts hold no weight. They no longer exist. When awake, we see others in truth; we are no longer enmeshed in the thoughts woven into our minds. This is difficult and uncomfortable at first.

Old Foe

An unmet need,
Old foe Conflict raises its head
The hunger for something
Remains unfed

Layers of lenses
A bridge to connection
Trauma and anguish
A vexing dejection

Choices and decisions
From a vagrant mind
Do we wrestle with the void
Or cast love aside?

Self-love and reflection
We cup our hands to drink
From an ancient promise
Of freewill in the world of think

Orphic Wonder

But to feel from the heart
To reach the part within,
Starved of love and understanding,
The soul becomes too thin

Stretch forth into love
That orbits without need
That fills the cup of you,
For it is you, you need to feed.

No more scraps from the table,
Or offcuts from the abyss
Just the simplicity of you
The clarity of bliss.

Witnesses

What is truth? Surely it cannot be grown from thoughts. Thoughts and perceptions can be deceptive thieves, wondrous creations, fierce protectors, and angered children. When we merge and comfort the little one within, we will hold their hand tightly and walk into truth.

Platform 22

But who are you? Who are you really?
You were once a child
Or at least smaller.

Cumbersome and laughing, so innocent,
Taken into adulthood
On a carriage. It was fast and frightening.

You should have safety
Whoever you were. The child.
Sitting, waiting, hoping.

In empty air and tear-filled puddles
The night grew big
Bigger than the promise of days

A little taller, stronger too
On top of your steps, Platform 22
Who are you now?

Loops

Misguided invitations can lead to loops of despair until the lesson is learned.

Day of Frogs

The basket weave came loose
On the day it rained frogs.
A storm, they said.
Horror-filled awe and shock

The thrill of such wonders;
No croaks or jumps.
The saltiness of ocean air
Fury of apocalyptic cry.

Mingled and surprised,
Suction of air,
Lily pads abandoned,
Grandma cried.

Mother laughed, sipping warm gin
Too long to drink, with bare feet.
Folded pyjamas, an empty bed.

I watched from the porch

KB Eliza

Splatter and mayhem, brown, green mud.
The end, the end, her wrinkled mouth sung

All I could do that night was play
With the straw-coloured threads
From a basket under the bed.

Neenish Tarts

Neenish tarts and library books,
afternoon naps,
praying for a parking space.

Mischief the cat scratched my hand
when I tried to play the piano.
Everyone hated that cat but you—
a hard taskmaster, you said.

I squeezed myself into dolls' clothes,
ripping the back seams;
it was the only time I saw you angry.

Teenage Love

Why was it that when we held hands, it felt like a puzzle, the pieces fitting together exactly as they should? But you didn't like holding hands; you said it made them feel suffocated. But hands don't breathe. 'Mine do,' you said—they were special. But when I found out your hands touched others, I wanted to break your fingers.

Blue Freckles

Sweet cigars, warm whiskey,
A bible next to the bed.
All the soldiers came tumbling down
Broken, twisted, angry, scared.
Where are you, my friend?

I covered the blows meant for you
Kissed your tears away.
I can still taste the saltiness.
The pain of shock and realisation
In one so small.

Tiny, pale, skinny
Blue eyes, once friendly, now hidden.
Little arms wanting,
now muscled and scarred
Anger reserved for me, not understanding
A blank page sits where the story was
Changed forever? Paused?

KB Eliza

The days grow longer, as does the chasm.
You may not ever know me yet
I see you; I know you; I love you
Always

Last Words

I remember when you screamed at me SHUT UP. We never spoke again.

Telephone

When I was small, I dreamt of a telephone ringing in an empty black room.
What if I told you that even when I screamed into the phone, no one heard?
But then one day, someone answered.

It was you.

We made words and worlds to dance in,
where my feet never got sore.
I still dream of telephones,
but the room is empty no more.

Ignition

The attraction of distraction, loud
In a world clattering, relentless—
Scared of hope, wary of the light
Of novel ideologies stirring quiet storms.
Inertia shattered by collisions unseen,
'Enough!' we scream into the void,
'No more!' our chests resound with beats.
Defaults fall like debris around our feet;
We claim our now, fervent and unrestrained.
Curiosity, our newfound compass,
Guides us—ignition of insight, fuelled and aflame.

Dilute

When we search and seek outside for the answers that can only come from a personal encounter and a connection within, we dilute the learning and delay the process of finding out who we are...really.

Burn Away

A star falls from the sky
Burns your hands to a crisp
Yet in your infinite wisdom,
Will you deny stars exist?

A second life, a new one
The old has burned away
Yet, with your fiery words,
You deny my love for the day.

A star falls from my eye,
Bringing beginnings, so bright
I stand in infinite wisdom
I will never conceal its light.

Guideposts

There are beautiful companions along the way, beacons, agitators, teachers, guideposts.

My Corinthian

Trouble comes, but you are not crushed.
You are confounded,
bewildered but not in despair,
You are hounded but never abandoned.
Knocked down but never
Devoured.
This is what it feels like to know God.

Seriously

It really hit me in the heart when you said that creating boundaries was the only way someone would take me seriously.

Tug of War

Push away
Pull my thoughts
Squeeze my memories
Break my plexus
Tingle my intuition
Change your address
Block me
Unfriend me
Love, I will send,
Hope, I will wish
Wellness, I will pray
Dust, I will shake from my feet
May we meet again,
Until then, thank you.

Storm

The storm rumbles above,
clouds moving fast,
like the spray of your words.
God calls me to take cover.
Breathe.
Under shelter I cannot see.

Do I trust the unseen?
Your absence may feel like the sun
has disappeared.
The rain comes,
cleaning my spirit.

The grass will grow,
flowers will bend to the heavens,
quenching their thirst.
The sun will emerge again,
and so, it is.

Longwinded

Do you ever feel like you over-explain just to avoid feeling misunderstood?

Keep Your Hands to Yourself

Are those hands clapping in applause?
Are they celebrating me?
Or do they belong to the men I trusted,
Who just
could
not
keep
them off me?

Are those fingers pointing the way,
Guiding me through the unknown?
Or are they pointing out blame,
Projecting
faults
that
aren't
my own?

Are those hands gently touching my arm?
Are they an extension of affection?

Orphic Wonder

Or do they belong to the frustrated,
Twisting
my wrists
too
tightly?

Are those fingers clasping a pen,
To write me a heartfelt review?
Or are they tapping out tyrannies,
Digital
darts
thrown
to
injure?

Are you playing hide and seek,
Or a pathetic peek-a-boo?
Behind those hands, your eyes reveal—
I
know
it's you;
I always
knew.

SShhhh

Silence is deadly, yet isn't it such a fierce protector?

Haunted House

Oh, how we danced and laughed,
you twirled me around, a magician.
'Have another!' An expensive elixir
appeared from your captive hands,
warmed my empty stomach.
Intoxicating, attentive,
I shone under your twinkling gaze,
feeling like a treasure. We retreated,
in your strong arms I drifted off safely.

Glorious friend became a thief,
my home so alluring,
yet you were not invited.
While I slept, you entered,
I awoke startled, shaken.
My kisses were not permission,
yet here you are, inside.

The small stone of stolen gratification
falls, an avalanche, breaking walls,

KB Eliza

shattering windows.
There's blood on the rug.
As the dawn comes,
memory like fog on a June morning,
the taste of shame on my tongue.

Sick for home, for my teddy bear,
teenage posters and the smell of pancakes.
Like spirits I cannot summon,
our eyes no longer meet.
Felt, unspoken, if challenged made real,
what am I now?
A taunting temptress, no—

I am a haunted house.

Treehouse

You hit me for crying but then built me the most beautiful treehouse in the world.
Grown ups were confusing when I was young.
But I learned a lot regardless, like stick around for the punishment; it might turn out okay.

Ambrosia

Sweet ambrosia of
potential,
seeping into my
reality.
A union so sweet to
imagine,
chemical spill into my mind.
Divine,
cover me in your golden
sunrise.
Lift me up into your diamond
dawn.

Romance of Words

Truth feels heavy, doesn't it? When we throw away the romance of words, things get real. Sometimes, it really feels uncomfortable. But discomforts have to be felt before we can sit in the weightlessness of peace.

Peanut Butter and Honey

You tied my shoelaces,
plaited my hair gently.
Your pillows scented with lavender
from your garden.

Pumpkin scones with butter melted,
tales of war romance,
a faraway look.
A dollar for ice cream,
a wink and a nod,
peanut butter and honey.

Magpies sang at your door,
knitting carefully folded.
Your love knew no limit,
no problem too large.

Your faith in a world of Goliaths,
your humanity edged with pride.
Steadfast judgement prised open

Orphic Wonder

with a mind eager to be unfolded.
Stubbornness and warmth,
made tender with a gentle fierceness.

You no longer tie my shoelaces,
you do not sit by my side.
The butter is no more,
knitting sits in the cupboard.
The pillowcase is stale.

Today I opened my door,
the garden grew lavender I did not plant.
A magpie sang for me.

Comedian

I wish I saw you sooner, but I was busy laughing at a world too silly to be taken seriously. Joking my way through trauma. Like a child with hiccups after too much lemonade.

So many manmade things taste so good but make you stick to the stomach. So now you've gone and I realise that whilst I like a good laugh, it shouldn't be at my own expense.

The Land of Grandmother

She kisses the wrinkled fingers
One by one.
Rheumy eyes, once golden,
Now knowing, shining.
Wisdom and sadness.
The goodbye is happening,
A journey will begin
She cannot be companion to.
No, no, no, she wants to stamp,
Shout, grab her body with hers,
Pull her close.
But this is like grabbing at smoke.
The journey is happening.
Her smile, her lap that held her head so well,
Her hand squeezes that spoke
A thousand words of comfort.
It is not over.
Your time together will change.
Time here, time there, worlds apart,
Yet the worlds will touch

KB Eliza

Once more, one day.
You will dance together
Beneath a limitless sky.
You will sing of all that was and will be
On grass so soft and green,
Where love curls around and within.
Eternity is a breath away.

Toe the Line

Tell me what you see—does it hurt your eyes?
tell me what you feel—would it come as a surprise?
ask if I need you—would you believe me if I lied?
ask me if I can heal, and why I always cry.

Push me to my limits—the sky can't stretch too far,
push me away again, into someone else's arms.
pull me into your shadows—the place where we can hide,
pull me into your games, so I can toe the line.

Secret place

Take me to the place where can tell each other beautiful secrets until the sun comes up. Where nothing can touch us but each other.

Dreaming

Was I sleeping all this way?
Was I sleeping through it all?
Was I sleeping when you yelled
and said you could take no more?

Was I sleeping as you bled?
Was I sleeping when you walked away
from everything we shared?

I'm awake now my darling,
I'm awake, where have you gone?
I'm awake and I realise,
I was dreaming all along.

Midnight Feast

Break past my defences into my heart in the only way someone called friend knows how. I will be waiting at the table with a bottle of wine and a midnight feast.

No Roses Today

Do not throw dirt upon her,
do not hand me a rose.
For the one I know and love,
is no longer there.
She is not in that gilded box — it is a shell,
a case you lowered
into the belly of the earth.

My beloved is not here,
I saw her take leave some time ago.
A wisp, and she was afar,
so fast it took my breath away.
The lights dimmed,
would they ever glow brightly again?

The sun is gone,
the rain has come.
Each tiny tick of my watch pauses.
So, do not hand me a rose.
Capture my memories with a snow globe,

KB Eliza

so I might shake it every day.
Each smile, each laugh,
each thought of her might float down.
I can watch it again and again,
so memories will not fade.

Alphabet Soup

PTSD the alphabet soup, with a sprinkling of Trauma Type C. What is this collective memory, that came back to haunt and taunt like bad reflux? Ah it can be rewritten you say? Punctuated and placed in a sentence that defines me to a world without baring my scars. An acronym for freedom in high definition.

Truth Shaker

Wild-hearted woman,
Where do you hide?
Do you consent to the
Lament of our fallen?
Or do you rise undisguised,
With a voice too loud,
With a stomp too heavy?
Is your intent to resent,
Or love your way through
This mire so dire and droll?
Is your destiny old and crone,
Or an elder of splendour?
There is no replacement
For complacence.
The price is far too high.
Your voice is strong,
Your stomp is thunder.
The time for masks is finished.
We do not exist to excuse,

Orphic Wonder

We are not curves to amuse.
We are the dream makers,
The truth shakers,
A creation meant for light,
The wild-hearted woman.

Upside Down

Sometimes when people pull away, it isn't because they don't want to see you. It is because they don't want you to see them.

Contortionist

False comfort comes
from pleasing others and squeezing yourself
into shapes to feel a sense of belonging.
Such actions won't feel comfortable for long.

This is the theatre of good intentions
made from the script of the subconscious,
and a tilt of your hat
makes for a demanding audience.

Your heart is too beautiful
to be stretched and twisted.
So, take a bow, exit the stage,
and enter the summer night.

Count

I don't like feeling this way, sitting in the fragments of my lesson. Like a maths class you don't like, but you have to learn it so you can count the money.

Child of Mine

Worn down child
Thrashing against convention
Trying to break free with words
Are you tired of breaking
Glass walls you put in place
Yet called them 'Others'
I know you
I understand you
Your intent is no mystery to me
It is a journey unfolding,
One we charted together
I am the universe
You are my child
If you allow it to be so.

Notes

The mind can muster an orchestra, yet you do not own a note.

The Roar

She cut the cord to set them free,
So, they could find who they needed to be.
They had not found the gold within,
Covered with moss and rusted sin.
They thought she was golden,
Too good to be true.
'I'll never be enough for the likes of you.'
So, they folded in half,
And folded themselves again,
Performing magic tricks
to make the world smile.
They didn't want to lose the light,
But too much folding comes undone.
They lay in the corner, exhausted.
She pleaded with them to have some fun.
They cried, *'Let us rest.'*
Her heart broke; what had she done?
Had she broken them, worn them out?
'No,' whispered her spirit,
'but you must let go.

KB Eliza

I've got you now; you will be safe,
But it is time, my love, you leave this place.'
She opened her eyes and saw the pain,
She roared into the wind,
'I will not ever do this again.'

Bin Day

Letting go and the need for detachment can be so difficult. I wish it were as easy as throwing out the garbage. But then, I was never very good at putting treasures I love in the bin.

Burleigh Heads

Rolling foam beneath my toes,
The crunch of memories
beneath my feet.
Are your ashes here,
ushered in by waves?

My skin warms to the touch of the sun,
as I lick salt from my lips.
Children run to their mothers,
squealing with fright and delight,
as the waves cheekily chase.

The gulls get closer, jumping,
a chip is stolen with a swift beak,
the paper is now soggy.
I smile.

You would let them eat
the chips all day long,
like lost long friends calling in for a beer.

Orphic Wonder

Washing our feet in the cool tap water,
sand stuck to our feet like glue.

Beautiful girls in gold bikinis,
a man was wearing one too.
You raised your brow that time.
'It takes all types, kiddo!
Wouldn't the world be boring
if we were all the same?'

Spreading your arms wide.
Beautiful sadness makes Sunday sweet,
on the Burleigh Heads beach.

Visitor

Foreboding Angst, where are you? Where have you gone? Down another rabbit hole?

No, Angst calls out; I have found a new home. You are left with calm and peace now.

Salt and Honey

friday nights are for fish and chips,
sundays for pikelets, buttery honey,
salt and vinegar.
we watch through sheer curtains
the chaos on the street at night,
fearing the knock
of a drunken stranger.
we leave fake names
to pick up potato cakes,
cut our hair differently
after licking honey from plates.
deadlocks on the door,
the manhole nailed shut,
like a crazed hedgehog.
this is to stop the one
who is not a stranger.
he won't knock
unless it's to drive some sense into us.
he won't cook
unless it's a scheme.

KB Eliza

he doesn't care for curtains,
prefers telephone books
to stop bruises.
the street chaos
doesn't compare
to what we left behind.
strangers are always
kindness in possibility.

Flattery

Please don't mock me with false words of flattery, glinting like jewels from the world's best thief. I never cared for blood diamonds.

Absurdity

They said *No*
They said *Can't*
They said *Or Else*
Do you shrink a little, retreat?
Perhaps you changed your path.
But was their *No* for good?
Was their *Can't* for you?
Did your path lead to the *Else* anyway?
Yes.
Because the plans you grow in the shadow
of others thwarts destiny.

Ribbons

When I get to heaven, they will marvel at the ribbons adorning my aura. What are they? They will oooh and aaah. Why these? These are the kindness of friends.

Grip

Did they snap your fingers
with their greedy grip,
demands so long, so far and wide?
What stories have they told themselves
about you?
You, they do not know
You did not write the chapters
A bystander has no place in hand holding
Burn the ships, sink the books
There is no going back.

Inquisitive

The unruly mind eventually eases in thinking and starts feeling.

Rose Coloured Glasses

I saw you through rose-coloured glasses.
I didn't mind one bit.
I didn't see your flaws,
for I adored you.

You left for those adorned with fancy bags.
One moment surrounded by so many of you,
then I learned a boundary or two.
It wasn't good for us, it seems.

I saw you growing, trying to be free
from a past punctured with trauma.
I didn't think that included me.

Now, with my vision clear, I walk,
reflecting on what was true.
Truth is a threadbare coat,
uncomfortable and itching.

Orphic Wonder

So I bid you farewell, my friend,
grateful for our history and time.
I too, must seek a different view,
as we part and find new covers.

Incite

When we anticipate the spark that will incite our lives, the months of collecting dead wood and searching in the dark will ignite our burning optimism.

Seasons

Sitting still beneath the tree,
I wondered what would become of me.
A brain changed, yet smarter still,
With intuition sharp.

Changed forever, not ungrateful,
Yet changed is changed, and different
Trees lose their leaves.
Would I lose friends the same way?
Time changes us all.
Would they fall, rot to the ground?

Or would they be evergreen,
Beautiful all year round?
Shade, lush, and green,
Holders of stories and afternoon picnics.

Virus

Treat others as you would like to be treated— now put THAT in a virus and watch the world evolve.

Fishing

You said you were going fishing,
But that wasn't quite true.
You were my protector, my pedestal.
Sweet cowardly lion, I love you so.
I wish you could find courage and grow.
Around the country, you travel
without care,
Forgetting the core you discarded.
Why can't you be alone for a while?
Find yourself and enjoy what lies within.
I do believe it is the quiet of your memories,
Stirred like old ghosts that keep you running,
Never looking back, never still,
Scared they will rise up and bite you
like snakes.
You have forgotten how loved you are,
Forgotten so much, it seems.
I love you still and always,
even if it's in between
Your drinking and laughing with friends.

Passports Please

There are more worlds to come my friend, this isn't the last stop. This world is called Learning. The next one is Eternal Life.

Checklist

What do you want to change?
The power others have over you?
To change the past, push the blame?
To feel authentically, without apology?
The cost is dear when we live
by others' expectations.

The price is just too high.
Yet, we look back at choices
and realise we had the power
to choose differently all along.

Freedom is a perception.
Our upbringing lends experience,
made and forged to survive.
These memories, shaped by time,
may need contemplation.

Reclaiming agency, standing in truth,
unapologetically alive.

Control Panel

I walk, I run, I see. I smile, I laugh, I read. I hug, I love, I dream. My brain is a wonderful thing.

All Silk and Whispers

You've carried me, always — a miracle of love.
My lessons hard earned, but here I stand,
ashes beneath my feet,
burned clean by your grace.
Beautiful doors open unexpected,
yet I know your signature calling card:
coincidence.
You save me again and again.

Shy light,
dodging drab,
all silk and whispers.
A pocket of wildfire for your thoughts,
the cryptic script of your words.
What tricks will you flip with those cards?
None with hearts.
Mundane,
beguile,
dip and trip—a disaster.
Brushes against my spine,

KB Eliza

Celestial, coaxing calm from chaos.
Gossamer,
nocturnal,
immense and intimate.
Arrested,
The true protagonist of minds,
like a million specks of shining soul dust,
exploding into overwhelming elation.

Home.

Margins

Wisdom waits for us all when we stop listening to the noise and sit in silence. You might glimpse into the margins and see that you are loved.

Doorways

The doorways into your life
must not be neglected.
Imperious or sacred,
edifying or destructive,
they require attention.

When trouble strikes
and the stench of trauma lingers,
from where did they enter?

You can converse on the grass,
palaver on the porch,
but permission is granted by default.

Inner sanctum,
guarded and revered,
requires vigilance and care.

To let in only those

who nurture and heal,
not harm or ensnare.

Vase

It's an awful feeling when you know your heart and you know how much you care about someone, but they decide to avoid, deny, and twist things around—like moulding clay into a misshapen vase to hold flowers. People often won't sit with their struggles; they change the narrative because they can't bear the thought that the problem lies within them, not you. So, these flowers bloom with colours and scents of "nothing to see here; it's them, not me."

Ride of Your Life

The world around us
turns and spins without your assistance.
The plants grow, and the animals thrive
without our footprint.

Nature is no happy friend
but an unyielding, beautiful adversary.
We live in a manufactured world
that traps and confines us in arrogance,
believing her to yield to us
so we might call her home or commodity.

Insanity.

We are gifted elements, wonder, heartbreak,
and magnificence to enjoy,
perhaps survive?
We seek more;
the constructs of a fractured hive mind.

KB Eliza

Look at the flames licking through trees,
sparked by our curious fire.
This is an adventure, make no mistake.
Hold on tight, children.
You're in for a ride.

Too Late

Too late. Two words, the terrible twosome forged in regrets and 'what ifs.' They echo in the quiet moments, haunting the spaces between breaths. The chances not taken, the words left unspoken, all crystallised in those two final words.

The Velocity of I AM

Listening to the greatest composers,
does their music fill you
with indescribable emotion?
A whisper can move mountains,
yet gets caught in your throat.

Is there a vastness you sense?
The tingle of goosebumps
when truth electrifies your body,
and the world feels like it will explode
from your fingertips,
blasting everything in its terrifying path.

Have you been lost in the eyes of a creature,
sensing 'more'?
When a bird tilts its head
in contemplation of you,
when ancient songs of wanderers
flip your heart,
the awe of sunrise from atop a mountain?

Orphic Wonder

This is me.

When dimensions collide and paradox forms,
we sit in the now,
rebelling against the past,
learning from history,
striving for more, but wanting less.

This existence we call humanity
is seasoned with pattern,
velocity, causal effect,
and the polite sparring,
shaking hands between
classic and quantum physics.

Aren't we all using probabilistic reasoning?
Uncertainty is life.

Ashes to Ashes

The stick in my hand was masterfully crafted by the chisel of time, each stroke carving out trauma, sanding down survival's rough edges. It has passed through many hands, each generation whittling away, turning it into a tool to measure worth and deliver pain.

They say it's my duty to pass this stick down to my children, to continue the tradition of hammering lessons into them. But I won't. My hand will guide the saw that severs old ties. I'll splinter it into kindling, fuelling a fire for a future where I can warm my hands. Then, I will scatter the ashes to the winds, where they may be turned into something new.

Ashes to ashes, dust to dust; in sure and certain hope of the resurrection of a life worth living.

About the Author

The year KB Eliza started to write stories was the year she tried to live in a treehouse. It was an unusually wet one, with thunder that made her dog shake. As a young child, she loved to escape into the dimension of storytelling, and she read literature to her dog to help with the shakes. This was also the year she experienced faith, hope, and a strong notion that there may be more beyond our world than we can perceive. A spiritual quest started, the muse for a life of metaphysical enquiry. Now the full-time Australian writer dedicates her time to simple living and extracting the thoughts and wonders that arrive most days, inspiring prose and heart filled pondering. Orphic Wonder is her second book of poetry.

You can read more from kb at https://kbeliza.com

facebook.com/writerkbelizaofficial
instagram.com/k.b.eliza
tiktok.com/@kbeliza

www.ingramcontent.com/pod-product-compliance
Lightning Source LLC
Chambersburg PA
CBHW011150290426
44109CB00025B/2555